AN ALPHABET OF ANIMALS

ISABELLE BRENT

First published in Great Britain in 1993 by
PAVILION BOOKS LIMITED
196 Shaftesbury Avenue, London WC2H 8JL

Designed by Janet James

A CIP catalogue record for this book is available
from the British Library.

ISBN 1 85145 9766

Printed and bound in Italy by
L.E.G.O.

2 4 6 8 10 9 7 5 3 1

This book may be ordered by post direct from the
publisher. Please contact the Marketing
Department. But try your bookshop first.

TO MY FRIENDS AND
ANIMAL LOVERS EVERYWHERE
AND TO ZEBEDEE,
MY CONSTANT INSPIRATION

ARMADILLO

An armadillo's most characteristic feature is its protective coat of jointed scales. When an armadillo is attacked, it rolls into a ball so that its head is hidden and only its scales can be seen. Armadillos have very strong claws, which they use to carve out underground burrows to live in. An armadillo will often build several nests and use them in turn, instead of having a single home. It sleeps in the daytime, after foraging for food during the night. Since 1930 armadillos have spread from Texas to most of the southern states of America. One reason for this may be that an increase in farmland has meant there are many more insects for the armadillos to eat.

BUTTERFLY

Butterflies are very gentle and delicate creatures, so delicate that they can die of exhaustion from being too active. They live for only two to eight months, and they rely on their bright wing markings (which often look like huge eyes) to make them seem larger and more dangerous to their predators than they really are. But butterflies are not as frail as they seem. They can travel for vast distances and at enormous heights – some Tortoise Shell butterflies were once found high up among the Himalayan Mountains. The smallest butterfly in the world is the Dwarf Blue, which is about as wide as a person's thumb; the largest is the Queen Alexandra Birdwing of Papua New Guinea, whose wingspan is greater than the height of this page.

C

CHEETAH

The cheetah is the fastest animal on earth. It can reach exceptional speeds over short distances in order to overtake its prey of antelopes, gazelles, and warthogs, though it tires easily. In England in the 1930s cheetahs were raced against greyhounds. Needless to say, the cheetahs won. Both female and male cheetahs go hunting, although the females usually hunt alone, while the males hunt in groups. A cheetah will often drag its kill to a hiding place before eating it, to protect it from hungry vultures. The cheetah relies on its spotted coat for camouflage, and the dark stripes that run from its eyes to its nose make it seem frightening to its prey and predators.

DOVE

The dove is a symbol of peace and hope, and is best known from the story of Noah's ark, in which a dove brings an olive branch back to Noah to show that dry land is nearby. The Egyptians certainly treasured doves, and built tiny castles out of mud bricks for them to live in. Today people often keep doves in decorative dovecotes. Doves are very good at finding their way. It is thought that they are able to follow the sun or react to the earth's magnetic field. The Arabs were the first to use doves as messenger birds. The longest such flight ever recorded was made by a dove, belonging to the Duke of Wellington, that flew from West Africa back to its home in England.

E

ELEPHANT

Five million years ago elephants were smaller than Shetland ponies and lived on the islands of Malta and Sicily. In early times elephants were used in battle to scare off the enemy, and could carry castles full of archers on their back. Today's elephants come from Africa and India. African elephants have the larger ears of the two, since they live in hot open spaces and their ears help them to lose body heat. Elephants have very thick skin, too thick for their enemies to bite through and yet sensitive enough to register an insect landing on it. Elephants are known for their long ivory tusks, but they have teeth as well and use up six sets of teeth in their lifetime.

FOX

Foxes are often thought of as cunning and wily animals. They have been hunted by humans for centuries and have developed many ingenious ways to escape foxhounds: they swim through rivers, run along railway tracks and roads, and dash through smelly farmyards so that their scent is lost. They have also learned how to survive in towns and cities by making their home in parks and churchyards and eating scraps of discarded food.

Foxes belong to the dog family, although they have many of the habits of cats: they flick their tails rather than wag them, hiss and spit, wash themselves all over, and have green eyes that reflect the light at night.

GIRAFFE

Giraffes are the tallest living animals. A fully grown giraffe is more than three times taller than the average door frame. Its long neck is essential for reaching the topmost leaves of the acacia bushes on which it feeds. However, it has only seven vertebrae in its neck, the same number as for a human being. Giraffes grow extremely quickly when they are young, and the height of a newborn giraffe can increase by one-fifth within a day of its being born. The speckled pattern of giraffe skin is as distinctive as a human fingerprint but does not often serve as camouflage, since giraffes don't stand still for very long. But they have good eyesight and a very strong kick to protect themselves against predators.

HUMMINGBIRD

The hummingbird gets its name from the sound that its wings make as it flies. It flaps its wings faster than any other bird – up to ninety beats per second. This means that it can hover and position itself in flight in many ways, more like an insect than a bird. Hummingbirds build cup-shaped nests the size of a thimble out of spider's silk, flower petals, down, and lichen. The nest is so delicate that the hummingbird must place small stones at its base to prevent the wind from blowing it away. When building a nest, the hummingbird hovers alongside without relying on a perch, which other birds would need.

I

IGUANA

Iguanas are reptiles found in North and South America, the West Indies, the Galápagos Islands, Madagascar, Fiji, and Tonga. They are strange-looking creatures reminiscent of prehistoric monsters, with their crests, scaly skins, spiked tails, and dewlaps. These features have developed for good reasons: some desert lizards, for example, have wedge-shaped snouts so that they can bury themselves in the sand when they need to cool down, and they have spikes on their feet to help them grip the sand when running. The spikes and scales of all iguanas protect them from predators, for they make the iguana difficult to attack, injure, or eat.

J

JAY

There are thirty-eight species of jay, the majority of which have brilliant plumage. Most jays come from South America, although some live in much colder regions, such as Siberia. The bulk of their diet is made up of acorns, which they bury in the earth to store for future meals. This habit helps to spread the growth of oak trees, since the jays don't always find all the acorns they bury. Jays are known for their boldness and intelligence, and they are very good at imitating other birds' calls. One jay kept in captivity learned to imitate nearly fifty sounds, including its owner's voice, a guinea pig, and a rattling bucket.

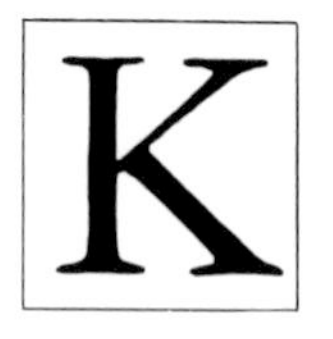

KOALA

Koalas may look like cuddly teddy bears, but they are neither bears nor cuddly. Like most animals, they can be very fierce when threatened, and they have sharp claws. They are a special kind of mammal known as a marsupial, and like other marsupials, such as kangaroos, their newborn babies live and grow in the mother's pouch for the first six months of their life. Koalas live in the eucalyptus forests on the eastern coast of Australia, where they feed on large quantities of eucalyptus leaves. Although they are very good at climbing trees, koalas are not very active and spend most of their time asleep – about eighteen hours a day.

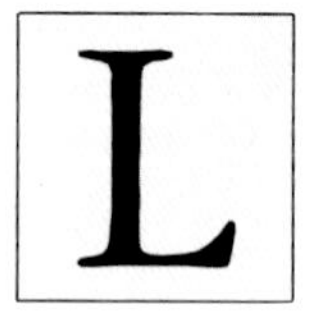

LION

Lions have long been called the kings of the animal world because of their courage, fierceness, and regal appearance. Rulers have often taken their names from lions, such as Richard I of England, who was popularly known as Richard the Lion-Heart, and Ali, the son of Mohammed, who was known as the Lion of God. Lions formed part of one of the first zoos: the Royal Menagerie, established by Henry I in thirteenth-century England.

Lions live in large family groups called prides. They hunt for their food but also scavenge from kills made by other animals. Like small cats, they have retractable claws and rough tongues, which help them to strip the last morsels of meat from a bone.

M

MOLE

The word 'mole' comes from an Old English word, 'mowdiwarp', which means 'earth-thrower'. Moles are indeed expert diggers; in twenty minutes of digging they can move fifty times their own body weight in earth. The earth they remove when digging their tunnels is heaped up in molehills, and extra-large molehills (called fortresses) help to protect the moles' nests in early spring. Moles live almost entirely underground, coming up to the surface only when looking for nest materials, or if food is short. They have very poor eyesight but a good sense of touch, and their pink snouts can detect air temperature and currents. They have good hearing too, particularly underground, where sounds are made louder by their tubelike tunnels.

NEWT

A newt is a species of salamander, which is an amphibian lizard, able to live on land or in water. Newts lay their eggs in water. These eggs hatch into tadpoles that live in the water until they become adults. Some species of newt remain tadpoles all their life, unless their water supply dries up; only then can they turn into adult newts, able to survive on land. Some salamanders have poisonous skin, and if threatened the lizard can roll into a ball and present its poison glands to the attacker. Legend has it that salamanders were monsters that lived in fires, which they quenched with the cold of their bodies. This explains why asbestos, a fireproof material, is sometimes called salamander's wool.

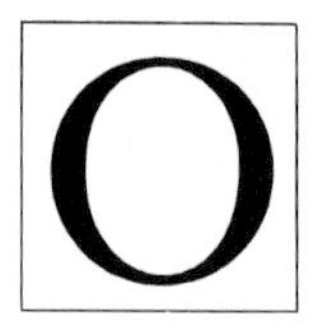

OWL

Owls are birds of prey that have developed intriguing features to make them excellent hunters. They can see at night a hundred times better than humans, and while their eyes cannot rotate very much, their neck can swivel very fast through three quarters of a circle. They also have superb hearing and can find and catch a mouse without needing to see or smell it. They are almost silent when they fly because of special filaments that grow on the edges of their flight feathers. When sitting still, they puff out their chest feathers as they breathe in, then pull them in when breathing out – so they appear not to be moving at all.

P

PARROT

The parrot's natural habitat is hot, tropical terrain, but parrots have been kept as pets for several centuries. They are exceptionally sociable birds and become very attached to their owners. They can be taught to imitate voices and have been known to memorize more than a hundred words, and to repeat entire sentences. The parrot is the only bird whose upper beak is hinged to its head, which gives it the power to crack even the hardest of nuts (not to mention people's fingers). This powerful beak is also used to grip and climb trees. One species, the Ground Parrot of Tasmania, can manage only short bursts of flight and, as its name suggests, lives mostly on the ground.

QUAIL

Quail are small, plump gamebirds, found mostly in Northern Europe. They migrate every year to central and southern Africa after their breeding season. Quail fly very little, preferring to walk through undergrowth or crops, where they find their diet of insects and grain and other plant foods. The mountain quail of North America has the shortest migration of any bird. In early September, when snow starts to fall on mountain peaks, groups of ten to thirty birds walk in single file down the Rocky Mountains of California. When winter is over, they walk back up the mountains to their spring and summer home.

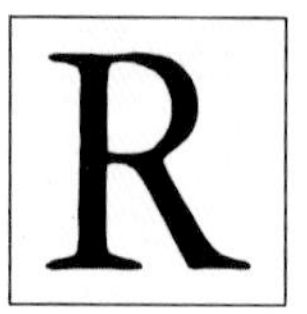

RHINOCEROUS

The rhinocerous is best known for its long horn, its weapon against predators. The length of this horn varies from species to species, and the Javan rhinocerous has no horn at all. The rhino's horn is also the reason it is threatened with extinction, for the horn is greatly prized in certain societies, causing poachers to kill a rhino for the money they can make from selling its horn. Rhinos have poor sight but good hearing and a strong sense of smell, which warn them of danger. One famous rhino, Cornelius from Canada, was made president of the Rhinocerous Party in 1979. His supporters claimed that he was an ideal politician, since he was thick-skinned and shortsighted, loved to wallow in mud, and was quick to run from danger.

S

SEAL AND SEA HORSE

Seals and sea horses are both marine creatures, but have little in common. Sea horses live in shallow, warm water and swim upright. They are the slowest-moving of all marine fish. The most unusual thing about them is that the male seahorse, not the female, carries the babies until they are born.

Seals live both on land and in water. Many species of seal live in very cold climates, such as the waters around the North and South poles, and are protected from the cold by their thick blubber. They are good underwater hunters because of their excellent vision, streamlined bodies, and their ability to close their nostrils and hold their breath for up to half an hour.

T

TOUCAN

The toucan is best known for its distinctive bill, which is made out of keratin, the same substance as human fingernails. It is hollow and much lighter than it looks, and is supported by a framework of small bones. It also has serrated edges for cutting food. A toucan uses its bill not only for eating, but also for preening, as a weapon, and as a way of recognizing other toucans. Its long bill enables the toucan to reach fruit and seeds on branches too thin for it to perch on. It then tosses the food back into its throat while gripping the branch with well-adapted claws: two fingers on each foot point backward and two point forward. The long bill is also used in play – to catch and throw pieces of fruit, and to wrestle with other birds.

U

UMBRELLA BIRD

This curious fruit-eating songbird lives in the tropical rain forests of South America. Its scientific name, *Cephalopterus*, means 'head wing', which comes, of course, from the large umbrella-shaped crest that is raised above the male bird's head in courtship displays. The males also make long, loud booming sounds to attract the females and show off their crest and the fleshy wattles that hang down from their chest. The most common species is the Amazon Umbrella Bird, which has immensely long tail feathers. The survival of the umbrella bird, along with that of many other creatures, is threatened by the gradual disappearance of the rain forests.

VULTURE

Vultures are best known for scavenging their food from the kills of other animals. Their hooked beaks are good for chopping but cannot cut through an animal's hide, so they have to eat from exposed carcasses left by other meat-eating animals. Vultures frequently go for long periods without eating, so when food is available, they often eat so much that they are unable to fly for a while. A group of vultures can pick clean the flesh of a carcass in about half an hour. Different types of vultures have different feeding habits. The Egyptian Vulture throws stones at ostrich eggs in an attempt to break them open. The Bearded Vulture feeds on bones – first it drops them on flat slabs of rock and then swoops down to pick up the splinters and the bone marrow.

WHALES AND WALRUSES

Even though it lives in the sea like a fish, the whale is a mammal. In fact, the Blue Whale is the largest of all mammals and can weigh as much as twenty-four elephants. Whales are long-lived and can survive for up to ninety years. They are able to travel very long distances – one species migrates six thousand miles every year, from the Bering Sea to California.

Walruses also are mammals. They live in Arctic regions and are at home both in water and on land, although they can only walk awkwardly, by balancing on their flippers. Their tusks help them to move across the ice and to hack out breathing holes when swimming beneath it.

EXTINCT

Many species have become extinct over the centuries, sometimes due to natural disasters, but often because humans have destroyed the animals themselves or the environments in which they lived. The dodo has become the best-known extinct animal because of its peculiar appearance. It died out in the seventeenth century, partly because the explorers of the time found it delicious to eat. But extinction is not a thing of the past. In 1987 the last North American Sea Sparrow died in the Disneyland theme park where it had been living, and a project in Mauritius rescued the Mauritian Kestrel from the brink of extinction when there were only seven of these birds left in the world.

YAK

Yaks live on the plains of the Tibetan Himalayan Mountains, which are just below the snow line, and in other elevated regions of Central Asia. To protect itself from the bitter cold, the yak has developed a coat hairier than that of any other animal, one that reaches all the way down to its feet. The yak feeds on lichens, tubers, and grass and has to find water to drink, since it cannot digest snow. Despite its large size and clumsy appearance, yaks are agile and surefooted when climbing across rocky ground. Some yaks can be tamed to provide milk, carry burdens, and pull vehicles like cattle. However, the largest species of yak, whose shoulders reach higher than the head of an average-sized man, is entirely wild.

Z

ZEBRA

Because of their distinctive striped coats, zebras were once called horse tigers by the ancient Romans, who kept them in circuses. Today, zebras live wild in large herds on the plains of Africa. The pattern of a zebra's stripes can indicate which part of Africa it comes from and to which species it belongs. Although zebras greet each other by sniffing one another all over, it has been shown that they rely more on sight than on hearing or smell to identify other zebras – which is another clue as to why they have distinctive stripes in differing patterns. The striped coat is also a form of camouflage, as the zebra does not appear to be a solid shape when viewed from distance in shimmering heat.